D1413614

WORK IT, GIRL

BLAST OFF INTO SPACE LIKE MAE JEMISON

Written
by
Caroline
Moss

Illustrated
by
Sinem
Erkas

Frances Lincoln
Children's Books

Chapter 1

Twinkle, Twinkle, Little Star

· · · · · · · · · · · ·

When Mae Jemison was a little girl, she dreamed of sailing off into space on a rocket ship.

> NO ONE IN HER FAMILY WAS AN ASTRONAUT OR TALKED MUCH ABOUT OUTER SPACE, AND YET MAE WAS LIKE A MAGNET, PULLED TO THE VAST WORLD JUST OUTSIDE HER OWN.

Dreaming big was not something a young Black girl from Alabama in the 1960s was encouraged to do. It was better to dream realistically. The civil rights movement was in full swing. It was radical to be Black and to be educated, to vote, or to work even the most run-of-the-mill job. It was not something to be taken for granted, especially if you were a woman of color, who was denied, somehow, even more rights than her fellow men of color. So, when it came to outer space, well, that seemed to be a world reserved for men—and white men at that.

Mae Jemison had a mom and a dad who had good jobs and who worked hard: her dad was a carpenter and her mom taught elementary school. But she could not find any women who looked like her in the field of space study. Discouraged? Maybe, a little.

Late at night, she would look up at the stars in the sky from her bedroom window, remembering the lullaby her mom used to sing when she was a kid. "Twinkle, twinkle, little star... how I wonder what you are."

> UP ABOVE THE WORLD SO HIGH, MAE THOUGHT SHE SAW A STAR TWINKLE JUST FOR HER. AS SHE CLOSED HER EYES AND FELL ASLEEP, MAE DREAMED ABOUT A FUTURE WHERE SHE JOINED THE STARS IN SPACE.

Sometimes dreams are dreamed very early on in life, but don't come to fruition until much later. No matter how much Mae loved space, she was only a young girl. As far as she knew, kids weren't allowed to go to space. When she told her parents her dreams, they did not

laugh at her or think she was silly. They, like Mae, took her dreams very seriously.

"You are going to have to work very hard," her mother, Dorothy, would tell her. "You are going to have to pay attention in school and always do your homework."

Mae would nod her head. Yes! She would always pay attention in school. She would always do her homework.

"You're going to have to prioritize learning, even outside of the classroom," her father, Charlie, said. "That means always remembering your big dreams and understanding that it takes sacrifices to achieve them."

Mae would nod her head again. Yes! She was willing to do anything for her dreams.

"As long as you believe in yourself, we will always believe in you," her parents told her.

Mae felt safe and loved and supported. These were the important seeds that she needed to plant in order to see her dreams grow.

"NO-ONE SHOWS A CHILD THE SKY."
African proverb (quoted by Mae)

Chapter 2

Everything Is SCIENCE!

· · · · · · · · · · · ·

Sometimes young people have hobbies or dreams that they grow out of or grow tired of. Though they never said so out loud, Mae's parents wondered if Mae's love of space was just a phase. Not so! Mae not only stayed focused on her love of the galaxies, Moon and stars, but she also took a liking to science and math.

'Phew,' her parents thought. Space was fun, but it's all about science and math. If Mae didn't flourish in those two subjects and genuinely enjoy learning in class, she would have a very hard time trying to achieve her goals. Impossible? No. Challenging? Yes.

Luckily, Mae already viewed the world through the lens of a budding scientist.

Born in the middle of October in 1956, Mae was the youngest person in her family. She was forever tagging along with her two older siblings—and would often get into scraps playing around outside in their Chicago neighborhood. Skinned knees and muddied clothes were not an unusual site around the Jemison house.

One afternoon after playing outside, Mae came running into her house shouting for her mother.

"Mom!" she yelled, "I got a splinter and I need help getting it out!"

Mae's mother came into the kitchen where Mae was standing, holding out a reddened thumb.

"Okay, Miss Mae," she said. "Let me find my tweezers."

Mae watched as her mother prodded the splinter out with the ease and elegance of a swan gliding onto a cool blue pond in summertime. She always knew what to do.

> "YOU KNOW," MAE'S MOM SAID, EYEING HER DAUGHTER, "EVERYTHING IS CONNECTED TO SCIENCE. LIKE THIS SPLINTER RIGHT HERE. THIS CAN BE SCIENTIFIC."

"I don't get it," Mae said. How could this painful sore on her thumb be science? She looked at her thumb, where a greenish yellow liquid (gross, but also fascinating!) was oozing out of where the splinter once was.

"Well, let's see. Isn't that interesting," Mom said as she inspected the gooey finger glop. "It looks like it might be a little infected!" She held up Mae's hand to show her. "This fluid is called pus."

MAE'S EYES WIDENED. SHE WANTED TO LEARN MORE. WHY DOES A BODY MAKE PUS? HOW DOES AN INFECTION HAPPEN? WHY DID IT HAPPEN TO HER? HOW WOULD SHE HEAL IT? DID SHE NEED TO GO TO THE DOCTOR?

"Pus?" It was such an... *unsavory* word, though she was also SO interested in the science happening right there, inside her body. She was hooked.

Her mom helped her do a science experiment with the infection, and she learned so much about doctors and science and health in her small study. Mae was also excited to realize this was something that truly interested her. She wanted to know everything!

Unfortunately, not every adult in Mae's life was as supportive as her parents...

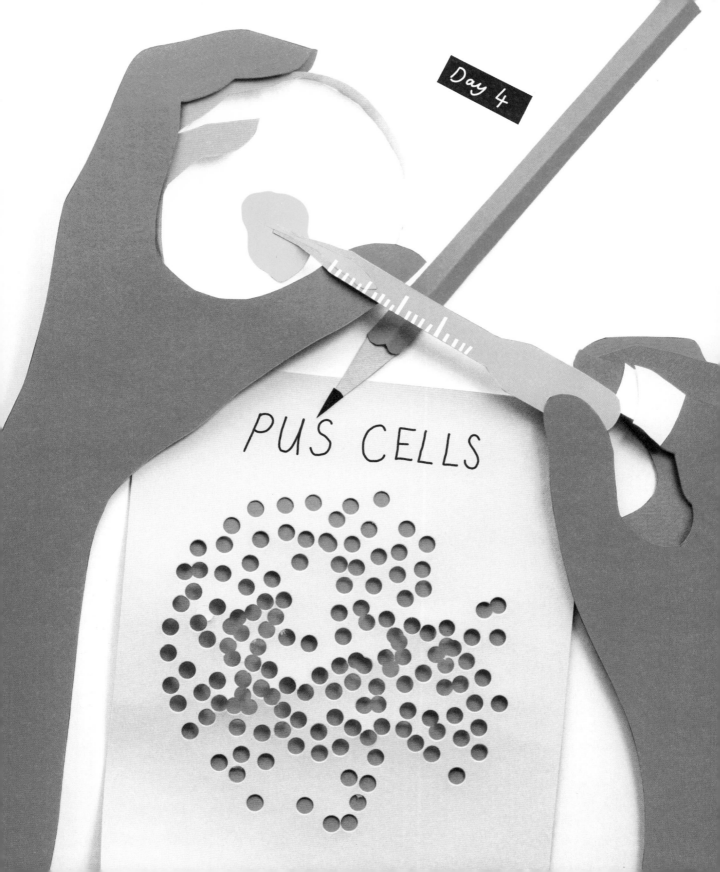

"NEVER BE LIMITED BY OTHER PEOPLE'S LIMITED IMAGINATIONS."

—Mae Jemison

Chapter 3

"Don't You Want To Be A Nurse?"

. . . .

After her at-home science experiment with her infected splinter, Mae was so excited to go to school and tell her teachers and classmates what she discovered. She was so excited, actually, that when her teacher happened to ask the class to think about what they wanted to be when they grew up, Mae's hand shot up immediately.

"Mae, yes, do you have a question?" her teacher asked.

Mae put her hand down and cleared her throat. "I know what I want to be. I want to be a scientist!" She sat up straight in her chair and smiled proudly.

All of the kids around her murmured.

"Cool!" they said.

Mae's teacher was quiet. She didn't smile or even semi-smile. She stood very still and her eyes squinted a little bit. She looked like she was thinking, Mae understood, but about what? Mae started to get nervous. Her hands started to sweat a bit.

"Mae," her teacher began. "That's a mighty big dream. Maybe you could be a nurse?"

A nurse??? Mae thought. *A nurse is a great job but it's not what I want to be!*

At first, Mae was so discouraged. Her teacher, whom she respected and looked to for guidance, thought she couldn't be a scientist. Maybe... maybe her teacher was right. There weren't many female scientists and there were even fewer Black female scientists. It would be really hard to make that dream come true.

> IT MIGHT EVEN BE AN IMPOSSIBLE DREAM. HER TEACHER QUICKLY CHANGED THE SUBJECT, LEAVING MAE FEELING A LITTLE SAD.

When Mae got home later, she slumped down in the kitchen chair and put her head in her hands.

"What is wrong, Mae?" her father asked. "You look sad."

"I don't think my teacher thinks I can be a scientist," Mae murmured. "But I don't understand why not."

"It does not matter what anyone thinks," Mae's mom touched her arm gently. "What matters is that you work hard, set goals, and do your best to achieve them. What matters is that you believe in yourself. We believe in you."

That made Mae feel way better. But she was still confused. Didn't teachers have big dreams for their students? And weren't the 1960s a radical time of change?

Mae kept her head down at school and studied hard. She participated in science fairs and learned more about how math and science fit together. When she was 9, something really exciting happened. It was announced that NASA, which stands for the National Aeronautics and Space Administration, was going to launch a series of trips to the Moon called Project Apollo. (Remember: no-one had ever been to the Moon before.)

Mae's mind was blown. This was happening. In her lifetime! She used to stare up at the sky and dream about space, but she never thought it was actually a place she could go. When the news stations aired the missions on television, Mae and her parents and siblings crowded around the small TV set in their Chicago living room. Mae stared at the screen. All she saw were white men in spacesuits. Once again, she felt discouraged... but she still couldn't take her eyes off the news.

Each night she'd go to bed and dream about a spaceship that would blast her into the sky. Each night she'd dream of a galaxy where people who looked like her were welcome and celebrated.

"I WAS REALLY IRRITATED THAT THERE WERE NO WOMEN ASTRONAUTS AND THERE WERE NO PEOPLE OF COLOR.

"I THOUGHT, WHAT IF ALIENS RUN INTO THIS CREW—THEY'RE GOING TO THINK THOSE ARE THE ONLY PEOPLE ON EARTH. I THOUGHT IT WAS UNREASONABLE NOT TO HAVE EVERYONE REPRESENTED."

—Mae Jemison

Chapter 4

Dancing Through Life

· · · · · · · · · · ·

When Mae turned 11, she had an opportunity to participate in an after-school activity of her choosing. She was already doing so much science both in the classroom and on her own time (it was her favorite hobby!) that she wanted to try something different.

She thought about sports, but she didn't much like sports. She thought about theater but sometimes she was shy about singing in front of a large audience. "How about dance?" her mom suggested. "You love to move and it's fun."

Mae decided she'd be willing to give dancing a shot.

She loved it! Oh my, did she love it. Mae became so obsessed with dance, she couldn't get enough. She took every class available to her. Ballet, modern, African dance, even Japanese dancing! Mae practiced really hard and decided she may have a new dream on her mind.

SHE WAS PRACTICING SO OFTEN, AND, MUCH LIKE HER LOVE OF SCIENCE, IT NEVER FELT LIKE WORK. IT FELT LIKE PURE JOY!

She loved leaping across the stage, moving her arms and becoming one with the music. Dance made her feel invincible. Plus, she was good! Her dance teachers marveled at her technique, presence, and work ethic. She felt proud of herself as a dancer. She was still getting straight As at school. Her parents were happy she was prioritizing school as well as dance.

"I WANT TO BE A DANCER," SHE ANNOUNCED TO HER FAMILY OVER DINNER ONE NIGHT.

Mae was now 14 and in high school. Auditions for West Side Story were the following week, and Mae was hoping to snag the lead role of Maria. She had been practicing really hard, putting in long hours in the dance studio after school and on weekends. She was one-track minded on this topic lately, listening to the music non-stop in her bedroom. She was starting to think about her future. She had seen a few older kids graduate high school and go to study the performing arts in New York or San Francisco. It looked like a lot of fun. It looked like

something she might want to do, too.

Her parents looked at each other warily.

"I thought you wanted to be a scientist?" her mom said between bites of food. "Please pass the pepper, Mae."

Mae handed her mother the pepper.

"I do. I want to do both, I think. I don't know. I love both science and dancing." Mae sat thoughtfully, looking down at her food. "Can people do both things?"

"YOU MEAN," MAE'S DAD ASKED, "CAN YOU BE BOTH A SCIENTIST AND A DANCER?"

"Yes," Mae said. "I guess what I want to know is: do you think I can be both?"

This was a tough question for Mae's parents to answer. They did not want to be the ones in charge of choosing Mae's destiny, and they had always promised to be supportive no matter what or who she chose to be. After a brief pause, Mae's mom nodded her head.

"Yes," she told her daughter. "I think—actually, I know—you can be both. But it's important to remember that you can always dance if you're a doctor, but you can't doctor if you're a dancer."

This made sense to Mae. It helped her to prioritize her goals and dreams.

She never did get the lead role in West Side Story at school. But she did get to be a principal dancer.

IT DIDN'T MATTER TO MAE, AS LONG AS SHE WAS ALWAYS SPENDING HER TIME DOING THE THINGS SHE LOVED.

Chapter 5

College At 16

• • • • • • • • • •

A few years later, a high school administrator called Mae's home. They wanted to speak to her parents. Mae got nervous. Had she forgotten a homework assignment? Failed a test? She could hear her parents both speaking on the phone in the kitchen, and crept downstairs for a closer listen.

Her hands were sweaty as she peeked through the banisters at her parents, sitting with their backs to her at the kitchen table.

"Okay, yes," Mae's mother said. "I understand."

There was a pause.

"Yes, I will speak with my husband and then we will both talk to Mae."

Mae's stomach dropped. She was so in trouble. But she could not for the life of her figure out what she had done wrong. Her parents huddled together whispering. Mae watched them for a minute, then thought she could make an escape. She tried running back up the stairs before her parents could spot her. No such luck.

"Mae, I can hear your footsteps," her father bellowed, laughing.

DARN IT, MAE THOUGHT, *BUSTED*.

She slowly walked down the stairs into the kitchen, trying her best not to look guilty.

"Mae," her mom said. "We have some interesting news."

Mae's eyes widened as her parents explained to her that the school had called to let her know that Mae had done so well in school and had completed so many of the necessary requirements for college applications, that she could actually start applying to universities now, at the age of 15. This was huge! This was bigger than huge, it was a massive, gigantic, wonderful honor. To graduate early was meaningful. Her hard work was paying off and others around her could see it. They believed in her like she believed in herself! But it also made Mae start to feel nervous. Most of the other kids at college would be older than she was. She might feel lost or confused or without a friend. Did she really want to take this big step?

"But...," Mae began. "That would mean I would go to college as a 16-year-old. Most students start college when they are 18. Won't I stick out like a sore thumb?"

"We talked about it," her father said. "But you've worked so hard. You

should continue to be able to expand on your education. Sticking out or fitting in is not what school is about, Mae."

Her father was right. She wanted to continue learning about science and space and math and the arts and she knew college would be an amazing place to continue that education.

Off Mae Jemison went to Stanford University, one of the best universities in America, at 16. She was enrolled to study Chemical Engineering and African American Studies. Other students and professors were awe-struck by this young woman on the college campus.

Mae did not have time to worry about fitting in or sticking out. Just like her father said! She was busy learning. She was studying chemical engineering and started to study other languages. She made time for dancing and the performing arts. She studied late and focused on her goals of flying into space on a rocket ship. She dreamed big, but she also worked

hard. Those things, she was learning, often have to go hand in hand for dreams to be achieved.

> **THE FOUR YEARS MAE SPENT AT STANFORD POSITIVELY FLEW BY, AS FAST AS A METEOR BURNING UP ON ITS WAY TO EARTH.**

One day she was a 16-year-old freshman, and the next she was 20 years old and debating where to go for medical school. Out of all of the schools in the country, Mae chose Cornell University in Ithaca, NY. It was much colder there than in Stanford, that was for sure! In 1981, she graduated Cornell as a Doctor of Medicine.

Her parents were so proud. Her teachers were so proud. Mostly, Dr. Mae Jemison was so proud of herself.

"JUST BECAUSE THERE'S NO-ONE ELSE DOING SOMETHING, DOESN'T MEAN YOU CAN'T BE THE ABSOLUTE FIRST ONE."

—Mae Jemison

Chapter 6

NASA Chose Me?

· · · · · · · · · · ·

Being a doctor was very fun. Mae thought about the science experiment she performed on her finger splinter back when she was a child, operating with tweezers. Now she was a real live doctor. A scientist! Her dreams were coming true all of the time...

For a few years after graduating from Cornell, she was part of the Peace Corps. Have you ever heard of the Peace Corps? It is where outstanding and accomplished Americans like Mae Jemison go to volunteer their services to countries abroad who need their help. Members of the Peace Corps focus on fighting things like AIDS/HIV, devastating sicknesses and starvation, and protecting the environment. Mae—now Dr. Jemison—felt very fulfilled by her work there, because she really loved helping others and seeing the world.

DURING HER TIME IN THE PEACE CORPS, MAE SAW AND LEARNED A LOT. COLLEGE MAY HAVE BEEN OVER, MED SCHOOL MAY HAVE BEEN OVER, BUT SHE WAS ALWAYS A STUDENT OF LIFE.

She learned different languages and became fluent in many of them. She also continued her love of dance! Phew. She was busy!

But as we all know, keeping herself busy did not mean she was too busy for her big dreams.

When Mae came back to America, she saw that NASA was accepting applications for astronauts. She thought about Sally Ride, a trailblazer; the first American woman in space. She was inspired.

Hmmm, she thought. She knew astronauts weren't just people who put on a big white spacesuit and got into a rocket ship. She knew they were scientists. And Mae was now a scientist herself. She had lots of experience—she was no longer a little girl just working hard for her dreams. She had already made so many of them come true.

Her dream of going to space was still as big and bright as ever.

Of course, Mae was nervous. It's always nerve-wracking to go for your dreams, right? The fear of failure is so palpable (that is a fancy word for "so close you can almost taste it") and Mae worried that if she applied and didn't get a call from

NASA

ASTRONAUTS
WANTED!

NASA that she would be so disappointed she might give up on her dream all together! It was also dangerous. Space travel was not to be undertaken lightly.

What was the alternative? To let the fear of striking out keep her from playing the game? Mae didn't think so. So, she mustered up all of her courage, and took a look at the NASA application.

Something she learned in school as a young girl—and as a scientist and doctor-in-training—was to read directions carefully and thoroughly, sometimes more than once before completing the task! As a kid, this was such a tedious task for Mae. That means it felt like it was making her work longer and harder and more boring. But as she grew older,

she realized this very good habit was helpful during test taking and doing her homework. As an adult, she learned how to do this with work and tasks. Mae was very careful and as a result, often very successful. Sometimes being too careful can stop you from going for your dreams. Mae still dreamed of sailing away on a rocket ship, up, up, up and away to the Moon and beyond.

Mae sat down at her desk and looked at the NASA application. It was long. Like, really long. They had a lot of questions. And Mae was tired!

The application asked about her education, what she studied and what her grades were. They asked detailed questions about her work in the sciences

and about the questions she wanted to focus on answering in her work at NASA. Everyone who wanted to hire for jobs, Mae was realizing, was very curious about the grades applicants received. *I'm glad I studied so hard*, she thought as she filled in the answers to the questions.

She looked at her calendar. It was September. The application said she may not hear back for a few weeks. Back then, there was no website she could check. Cell phones did not exist. She would have to wait by the mailbox until her letter from NASA arrived.

The weather turned from September heat to October chills, and people started taking in their beach umbrellas and trading them in for jack-O-lanterns and scary costumes and yummy candy treats. Still, Mae waited.

AND BOY, DID MAE WAIT. SHE WAITED PATIENTLY AND SOMETIMES NOT SO PATIENTLY.

Finally, in the middle of October, the mailman approached Mae's mailbox carrying one sizeable manila envelope with the return address clearly stating NASA...

Mae grabbed the envelope right out of the mailman's hands and tore it open right there on the spot, scanning the letter with her eyes.

> **"DEAR MISS MAE JEMISON," MAE MURMURED, READING THE LETTER, "...WE ARE PLEASED TO INFORM YOU THAT YOU HAVE BEEN ACCEPTED TO TH--."**

Mae screamed and jumped up and down. She was accepted! Out of 2,000 people, she had been accepted to the NASA astronaut program! NASA chose her! Oh my gosh! The mailman looked at Mae like she was crazy but was equally as thrilled when Mae explained why she was so excited.

"You're going to go up into space in a rocket ship?" he asked.

"I sure hope so!" Mae exclaimed.

Mae realized quickly that out of the fifteen people selected for the 1987 NASA program, she was both the only Black person and the only Black woman. In fact, there were only five Black people at NASA, and all of them were men. If this program was going to require a lot of work from everyone who was accepted, it would require even more work from Mae. Black people were not given the same opportunities white people were. Black people were not automatically respected and trusted like white people were. Systemically, colleges and big corporations alike were biased towards applicants. It was an accepted practice at the time to judge applicants by the color of their skin—with white skin preferred by institutions. If you were Black, you had to work extra hard. Though unfair, some of that stigma is still true today. It's called racial bias, and it is deeply rooted in our culture and world. So much so that it takes time, effort, and work to unlearn that bias. Mae knew she was going to really have to work; work harder than she had ever worked before, and we all know Mae was used to working very hard.

It didn't matter. This was her dream. She was going to do whatever it took. "The thing that I have done throughout my life is to do the best job that I can," she told *Ebony Magazine* in 1987.

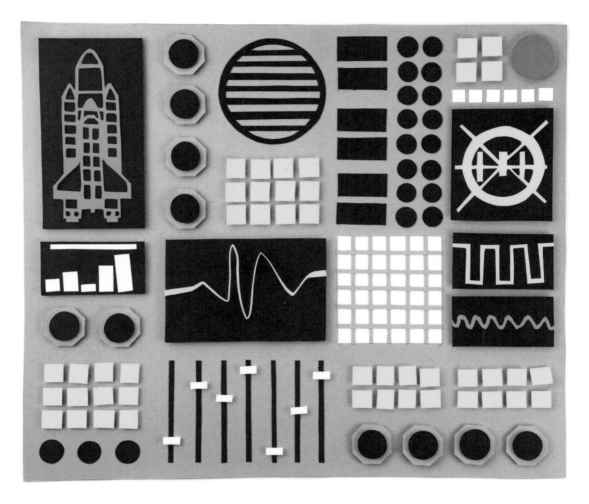

Mae started her training to be an astronaut. She hit the ground—and the books—running. She was in the front row during every class, took copious notes, and asked lots of questions. She got a restful night's sleep most every night and ate healthy meals to keep her energy up. She wasn't perfect—no one is—but she was so driven that she gave it 100 per cent every day. An admirable quality in anyone!

One year later, Mae had finally completed her training program as a mission specialist with NASA. It was 1988, and she landed a role in the Cape Canaveral, Florida, Kennedy Space Center. Her new job involved using her math and science knowledge to work with software for shuttles. She loved it so much. It made her so happy. She was still on the ground but she'd often look up at the Moon and the stars at night, knowing one day she'd be up there, joining them in their dance across the sky.

Chapter 7

3, 2, 1 . . . BLAST OFF!

· · · · · · · · ·

Mae, also known as Dr. Jemison, was on top of the world both literally and figuratively. She was living her dream each and every day. She was so happy that her hard work had paid off, but it seemed there was still lots of hard work left...

For a full year after she was accepted into the space program at NASA, Mae was in rigorous training. Think about something you learned to do. Maybe it was riding a bike, or learning how to play a sport, or singing a song. You had to learn first... before you could do. Practice makes perfect, and before Mae Jemison could soar to the stars,

she needed to train for that very special moment.

A lot of her training was in a classroom, but sometimes she got to go into a makeshift spaceship. It looked just like the real spaceships she'd one day be in, but they were built to be indoors so astronauts could learn and train in a safe and familiar environment. She learned how to work in zero gravity conditions. Have you ever tried doing your homework while floating in the air? It's way harder than it looks! Mae had to learn how to eat, drink, type information, measure things, write research... all floating in the middle of the room.

The year of training for space went by so fast. She made lots of friends and really enjoyed learning from her teachers at NASA. But she was ready.

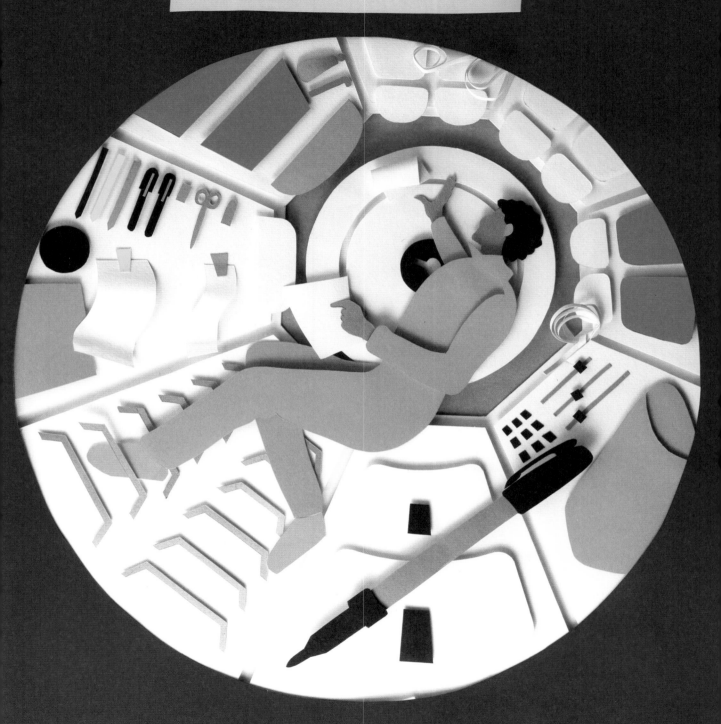

Ready to blast off into space...
Finally, it was time! All of her hard work was about to pay off. On the morning of September 12, 1992, Mae Jemison's dreams came true. She woke up early, far before her alarm clock went off. She took a shower; the last shower she would take on Planet Earth for about a week. She was so excited she was practically jumping out of her skin! She was going to space...
TODAY!

The space shuttle *ENDEAVOUR* launched out of the Kennedy Space Center, in Merritt Island, Florida, making Mae Jemison the first Black woman in space—ever. It was an historic day not just for Mae herself but for Black women everywhere. It was a huge trailblazing event and many people tuned in to pay witness.

All over the country, little girls turned on their televisions to see a woman in space who looked just like them. Dreams were coming true for Mae, and new dreams from new little girls were just beginning to plant their seeds. In an interview with the *Des Moines Register* on October 16, 2008, Jemison said that she was not driven to be the "first Black woman to go into space."

> **"I WOULDN'T HAVE CARED LESS IF 2,000 PEOPLE HAD GONE UP BEFORE ME... I WOULD STILL HAVE HAD MY HAND UP, 'I WANT TO DO THIS.'**

Little girls looked at Mae Jemison and thought, *that could be me!* Mae Jemison was off to the stars... and the journey had just begun. Everyone on Earth was cheering her on.

JUDITH
JAMISON

A.K.A Sorority

A K A

"I THOUGHT IT WAS IMPORTANT TO TAKE TO SPACE WITH ME THINGS THAT REPRESENTED PEOPLE WHO SOMETIMES ARE NOT INCLUDED."

Mae Jemison

Bundu Sculpture

Chapter 8

Dreams Are Out Of This World

Space is awesome. What have you learned about space?

You know that there are planets, and they orbit the Sun. You know that you need a special (and very expensive) spacesuit to go into space, because of the way the air and elements change as you go higher and higher into the air. You know that we live on Planet Earth, but that there could be life elsewhere. You know there are stars and suns and moons in the galaxy and that astronauts experience weightlessness or free fall when they are in orbit.

Let's talk about "microgravity" for a minute. Have you heard of that word before? Maybe you have in science class! But let's break it down. You've probably seen photos of astronauts in space, doing flips in the air like they're in a pool (COOL!). What's happening in that picture? You might be quick to say they're in a "zero gravity" environment, but that wouldn't totally be the truth. According to NASA, those astronauts are experiencing what's called "microgravity"—which just means that the amount of gravity in a specific space is very little (that's what the "micro" means!) but it's not technically at zero. Microgravity does funny things to your muscles and bones, which is why astronauts do experiments in space. Pretty cool, huh? Guess what? Some adults don't even know that!

And did you know that the food you eat in space is different than the food on your dinner table each night? If you have ever tried eating spaghetti and meatballs in microgravity you understand what we mean! (And if you have ever done that, we want to hear that story!)

Astronauts bring freeze-dried food with them to space. Mae loved the berries and the cheese the most. It was crunchy and sort of tasteless, but it got the job done. She felt fed and happy. Besides, her adrenaline was on fire! She couldn't think about silly things like eating. She was too excited; she was jumping out of her skin — oops, we mean spacesuit!

Mae was scheduled to be in space for eight days, a little over one week. Wow! That would be a really nice relaxing vacation, except she wasn't going to the beach. What was Mae doing up in space for eight days?

Let's take a look.

According to her own documentation of her space travel, Mae was a mission specialist who worked on investigations of bone cell research experiments. She also conducted experiments dealing with motion sickness—including the motion sickness experienced by the crew and herself. Now that's science!

SHE ONCE SAID, "PEOPLE ALWAYS THINK OF TECHNOLOGY AS SOMETHING HAVING SILICON IN IT. BUT A PENCIL IS TECHNOLOGY. ANY LANGUAGE IS TECHNOLOGY. TECHNOLOGY IS A TOOL WE USE TO ACCOMPLISH A PARTICULAR TASK."

Inside the space shuttle, Mae slept in a sleeping bag—just like you would if you were camping in the woods or sleeping over at a friends' house. But Mae's sleeping bag was strapped to the wall! This helped keep her from floating around and bumping into things while she was catching Zzs. Kind of funny, right? When she needed to use the bathroom, she would use a tube that would suck away body waste like a vacuum. It sounds pretty crazy, but astronauts are trained for crazy, since space is very different than being on Planet Earth. Aboard the shuttle there are lots of computers, servers, and workstations. After all, Mae and her fellow astronauts aren't taking a vacation to space; they're working on research projects to bring back after their mission and further space exploration for generations to come.

It was hard work for Mae and for her colleagues to complete all of their research, but we all know how it feels to achieve your dreams... it often doesn't feel like work at all.

On her only space mission, Mae spent 190 hours, 30 minutes, and 23 seconds in space. She didn't take one single second for granted.

STS-47
Mission: Spacelab-J
Space Shuttle: Endeavour
Launch Weight: 258,679 pounds
Launched: September 12, 1992, 10:23:00 a.m. EDT
Mission Duration: 7 days, 22 hours, 30 minutes, 23 seconds
Miles Traveled: 3.3 million

Astronauts sleep "standing up" in special sleeping bags and pods.

Space toilets work by using air flow. There are different tubes for number 1s and number 2s that suck waste material away. You have to use them very carefully!

You don't have any sense of being upside down in space. The floor can become the ceiling depending on your position in the spacecraft.

In microgravity, heavy equipment is easy to move with just your fingertip.

The crew onboard *Endeavour* were divided into red and blue teams to perform experiments around the clock.

Their test subjects included: the crew, Japanese koi carp, fruit flies, fungi and plant seeds, and frogs and frog eggs.

"I LOOKED DOWN AT CHICAGO AND I THOUGHT ABOUT
THE LITTLE GIRL WHO ASSUMED SHE WOULD GO INTO SPACE.
WHAT WOULD MY YOUNGER SELF HAVE THOUGHT IF SHE HAD MET ME?
I THINK SHE WOULD HAVE BEEN TICKLED."

—Mae Jemison

Chapter 9

Other Girls Like Me

· · · · · · · · · · · ·

After five years at NASA, Mae eventually decided it was time to move on and teach students who had the drive, the ambition and the dreams to also be scientists.

Do you remember Mae's second grade teacher and what she said to Mae? When Mae said she wanted to be a scientist her teacher cocked her head and said, "Don't you mean a nurse?" Whew. That stung like a bee. Why? Because she wanted to be a scientist and her teacher should have immediately supported her dreams and ambitions just like her mom and dad did.

Her teacher saying those words to her at such a young age definitely affected Mae. She did not let it discourage her, however, and she often wished she could go back to that teacher and let her know that Mae did become a scientist. But it's very likely that her teacher already knew what became of her student, because Mae Jemison was a well-known name thanks to being a trailblazer in the world of science.

Mae had never set out to prove her teacher and other naysayers wrong. It was never an anger that she held to tightly. Instead, it really made her think about the ways in which adults can affect kids with even the simplest or slightest of comments. Mae knew that her teacher wasn't trying to hurt her feelings or put her down, but rather she was speaking from experience. At some point in her life, Mae's teacher had probably learned that women did not have the opportunities that men had in the world of science. It was only natural that she was going to regurgitate that worldview in the classroom. Mae was happy not to have listened. It's important to realize that it wouldn't be 100 per cent fair to blame her teacher for her rude comments about Mae's dreams. In the early 60s, it just wasn't plausible that a woman would grow up to become anything she wanted. Women had specific jobs—nurses, secretaries, teachers—and that was about it. To dream bigger would be a frivolous activity; a waste of time. It would be far more productive to focus on the dreams that actually could come true. But Mae knew the truth at a young age: when you dream big and work hard, with the right support, anything is possible. The same goes for young girls and boys today. You can be anything you want to be, and do anything you want to do, as long as you work hard to achieve it.

MAE JEMISON FELT A PULL INSIDE OF HER TO GET IN FRONT OF YOUNG PEOPLE TO IMPART THIS WISDOM. SHE WANTED TO CREATE A BETTER WORLD THAN THE ONE SHE LIVED IN AS A LITTLE GIRL. SHE WANTED KIDS, ESPECIALLY GIRLS, TO KNOW THAT THE WORLD NEEDED THEM, AND THE WORLD OF SCIENCE DEFINITELY NEEDED THEM.

After a few sleepless nights, Mae finally decided what she'd do next. The Dorothy Jemison Foundation For Excellence, founded in honor of Mae's mother, was started soon after Mae left NASA.

"MY PARENTS WERE THE BEST SCIENTISTS I KNEW," JEMISON SAID OF THE FOUNDATION, "BECAUSE THEY WERE ALWAYS ASKING QUESTIONS."

Mae started The Dorothy Jemison Foundation For Excellence to inspire little girls to dream big dreams. Even though she never set out to be the first Black female astronaut, she still was, and she achieved more than she ever thought possible when the space shuttle went 3... 2... 1..., liftoff! She wanted other girls to see their potential and find their place in the world of science. Mae knew that including the voices of smart girls and women would greatly expand our knowledge as a collective whole, and that made her so excited.

The Foundation had a branch called The Earth We Share, which was a camp-like program focused on science experiments and projects for students ages 12-16. They spent four weeks learning about the world around them and how they can create and contribute to it being a better place for themselves and their communities. The participating students from all over the world work to solve problems that directly affect climate change and the economy. More importantly, they learn first-hand that science really affects everything in their worlds one way or another. Mae wanted young women all over the world to look to her and know that their dreams didn't have to just be dreams. That they could be real. Now that she had achieved her own dreams, a new dream was taking flight...

"WHEN I'M ASKED ABOUT THE RELEVANCE TO BLACK PEOPLE OF WHAT I DO, I TAKE THAT AS AN AFFRONT.

IT PRESUPPOSES THAT BLACK PEOPLE HAVE NEVER BEEN INVOLVED IN EXPLORING THE HEAVENS, BUT THIS IS NOT SO.

ANCIENT AFRICAN EMPIRES
—— MALI, SONGHAI, EGYPT——
HAD SCIENTISTS, ASTRONOMERS.

SPACE AND ITS RESOURCES
BELONG TO ALL OF US,
NOT TO ANY ONE GROUP."

—Mae Jemison

Chapter 10

Giving Back by Looking Forward

· · · · · · · · · · · ·

One of the most important qualities of a trailblazer or a leader is their ability to give back to those who haven't been as fortunate. In Mae's case, she knew she wanted to be a beacon of hope for young girls entering the male-dominated world of the sciences. As a child, she had a hard time finding people who looked like her who were also succeeding in STEM subjects (that stands for Science, Technology, Engineering and Mathematics!).

> **WHEN YOU DON'T HAVE A BLUEPRINT FOR YOUR DREAMS, YOU OFTEN HAVE TO CREATE ONE YOURSELF.**

That can be doubly hard work! Mae wanted to pave the way for another generation of young girls; to lighten their loads and give them more time to concentrate on making tomorrow brighter and better than today. She wanted to stand in front of young girls as proof that it could be done!

Mae was very focused on creating the future. She knew that was the best, and most meaningful, way she could give back to her field. She didn't think just in terms of her lifetime, she thought in terms of the lifetimes of people who weren't even born yet. She knew first-hand from working in the field of space that the world was vast and she was but a tiny speck within that vast galaxy. She would do her part to contribute to it in a productive manner.

In 2010, Dr. Jemison and The Dorothy Jemison Foundation were awarded the opportunity to lead NASA's 100 Year Starship Program. This was a huge deal! If you're wondering what that means, here's a simple way to describe it: one of NASA's biggest topics of research is interstellar travel, which is the ability to travel really, really, really fast to explore solar systems outside of our own. Right now, even though our space technology is impressive and advanced, we are still a way away from being able to visit other solar systems. The 100 Year Starship program was designed to instill research teams that would span over multiple generations, laying groundwork for the research teams that would take over long after the first team retired from the job. Ideally, within 100 years, interstellar travel would be possible because of 100 years of researchers! This was totally in line with Mae's passion, and she was so excited to win the opportunity to lead it to success, even if she knew it meant she would not be alive when the program was completed. Why, in 2019 we saw the first-ever photo of a black hole. Over 100 scientists worked together to make that photo possible. Wow!

MAE LIKED TO CONTRIBUTE TO WORK AND PROGRESSION THAT WOULD LIVE BEYOND HERSELF—BEING INVOLVED IN THE 100 YEAR STARSHIP PROGRAM WAS PROOF THAT IT WAS A DEEPLY ROOTED PASSION.

Beyond space, which was obviously a huge passion of Mae's, she also seemed to have a deep understanding that so many of the world's social, economic, and global problems were in desperate need of science and critical thinking in order to be fixed. Part of Mae's life mission was to help teach those around her—whether children or adults—to assess the problems surrounding them and work to create solutions.

Remember when Mae got a splinter and her finger starting oozing gooey pus (how could you forget?). That was science! Science can be found anywhere, and it can be found in the solutions to some of the world's biggest problems. That's what Mae wanted to leave as her legacy. "We need to use all the talent we have available to use to solve the world's problems," Dr. Jemison has said.

Today, the legacy Mae hopes to leave is one that exudes ambition and dreams; one that is so contagious that young women everywhere can't help but want to follow her lead and start innovating and creating and planning to change the world around them.

Mae Jemison sees herself and her work much like she sees the stars in the sky. One small bright speck in a sea of many, who combined with thousands of other small bright specks in the sky can make up something really big and important.

Blast Off Into Space Like Mae!

10 key lessons from Mae's life

1

DREAM BIG! Mae Jemison dreamed bigger than the stars and the sky. There is no limit to who or what you can be. Imagine that there was absolutely no limit to your dreams. Make those dreams your reality by writing them down and reminding yourself of them often.

2

The world around you will often teach you the best lessons. When Mae was little, she got a splinter stuck in her hand. It was then that her mom taught her an important lesson: science is everywhere! Mae did an experiment on her infection and learned a big lesson outside of the classroom. Learning can be done everywhere and anywhere.

3

Don't let the opinions of others determine your future. Mae's 2nd grade teacher shot down her dream of being a scientist when she told Mae she should think about being a nurse. If anyone tells you that you won't be able to achieve something, know that you can prove them wrong. Someone else's opinion has no bearing on what you can achieve.

4

There is no limit to the things you can be passionate about. Mae loved dancing and science and spent lots of time concentrating on learning how to excel at both. Eventually you may have to make a choice about where you want to focus most of your time and studies, but it won't be for quite a while. Try different things and see what you love.

5 **Work hard and take risks.** Mae Jemison worked so hard that she was able to graduate school early. She was excited but also scared. She knew this would be a risk. Eventually that risk paid off. Venturing outside your comfort zone is how you can truly accomplish great things.

6 **Stay motivated but remember it's okay to take breaks.** Dr. Jemison always had her dreams front of mind. But that's not always the case for everyone. To stay motivated, it's important to take a rest every once in awhile. Work and play are both important.

7 **Think about the things you can do today to help make tomorrow a better place.** Mae lived her life with a focus on making the future better. She knew that her work could help change the lives of people who would follow in her footsteps. For people who weren't even born yet, just like you. You can do the same!

8 **Keep asking questions.** There is no such thing as a stupid question. Questions can unlock new worlds, and there is no limit to the number of questions you can ask. If someone doesn't know the answer, visit your library to see if there is a book that can help you. A librarian would love to help.

9 **Travel and learn outside of your bubble.** We all live inside of our small worlds. Venture outside of what you know so you can learn more. Listen to people who live and play and think differently than you do.

10 **Honor the people you love.** Mae worked hard to achieve her dreams, but she always knew she had the support of her parents. Mae always thought about the family and friends who never let her give up on her dreams; always knowing her success belonged to not just herself, but to all of those people.

Grab a sheet of paper & a pencil and answer these questions!

Like in the experiment she did on her infected splinter, Mae found science all around her once she started really paying attention. Where have you seen science in your own life? Tell us about it!

• • • • • • • • • • • •

Mae had lots of passions—she loved science and dancing the most. What do you love? Make a list of all of the things you love—it can be as long as you'd like!—and put little stars next to your top two. What made you choose those?

• • • • • • • • • • • •

Mae knew in order to achieve greatness, she would need to stay motivated. How do you stay motivated to do your very best? Remember: There are no wrong answers!

• • • • • • • • • • • •

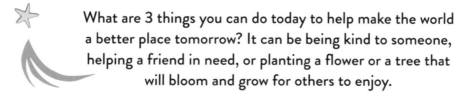

What are 3 things you can do today to help make the world a better place tomorrow? It can be being kind to someone, helping a friend in need, or planting a flower or a tree that will bloom and grow for others to enjoy.

• • • • • • • • • • • •

Mae always knew she wanted her legacy to be a great one. What will your legacy be? Why is that important to you?

Further Reading

Take a look at these other great books and resources to learn more about Mae Jemison. You can also read about and help the organisations she supports, or has founded, listed below.

Books
Mae Among the Stars by Roda Ahmed and Stasia Burrington
Women in Science: 50 Fearless Pioneers Who Changed the World by Rachel Ignotofsky
Mae C. Jemison (Women in Science and Technology) by Meeg Pincus and Elena Bia
Find Where the Wind Goes: Moments from My Life by Dr. Mae Jemison
The 100 Year Starship (True Books: Dr. Mae Jemison and 100 Year Starship) by Dr. Mae Jemison and Dana Meachen Rau
Exploring Our Sun (True Books: Dr. Mae Jemison and 100 Year Starship) by Dr. Mae Jemison and Dana Meachen Rau
Discovering New Planets (True Books: Dr. Mae Jemison and 100 Year Starship) by Dr. Mae Jemison and Dana Meachen Rau
Journey Through Our Solar System (True Books: Dr. Mae Jemison and 100 Year Starship) by Dr. Mae Jemison and Dana Meachen Rau

Online
TED Talks: Mae Jemison: Teach arts and sciences together
100 Year Starship
NASA
Exploratorium
Smithsonian National Air and Space Museum

Organisations
The Dorothy Jemison Foundation for Excellence
The Earth We Share (TEWS) Science Camp
Flying Doctors of East Africa
The Bayer Corporation

Work It Girl: Mae Jemison © 2020 Quarto Publishing plc.

Text © 2020 Caroline Moss. Illustrations © 2020 Sinem Erkas.

First Published in 2020 by Frances Lincoln Children's Books, an imprint of The Quarto Group. 400 First Avenue North, Suite 400, Minneapolis, MN 55401, USA. T (612) 344-8100 F (612) 344-8692 **www.QuartoKnows.com**

The right of Sinem Erkas to be identified as the illustrator and Caroline Moss to be identified as the author of this work has been asserted by them in accordance with the Copyright, Designs and Patents Act, 1988 (United Kingdom).

ISBN 978-0-7112-4515-0

The illustrations were created in paper

Set in Brandon Grotesque and Bebas Neue

Published by Katie Cotton

Designed by Sinem Erkas

Paper Modelling by Sinem Erkas and Christopher Noulton

Paper Assistants: Tijen Erkas, Nick Gentry, Lora Hristova

Edited by Katy Flint

Production by Nicolas Zeiffman

Manufactured in Guangdong, China CC112019

9 8 7 6 5 4 3 2 1

Photographic acknowledgements p34: African-American NASA astronaut Mae Jemison, 1991 © copyright Afro Newspaper/Gado via Getty Images. p38 top: NASA STS-47 Spacelab-J mission astronaut Mae Jemison has her spacesuit checked for leaks prior to the Space Shuttle Endeavour launch at the Kennedy Space Center Operations and Check-out Building September 12, 1992 in Merritt Island, Florida © copyright NASA Photo / Alamy Stock Photo. p38 bottom: Endeavour II space shuttle STS-47 insign © copyright Time Life Pictures via Getty Images.